How Things

Grapes to Raisins

By Inez Snyder

Children's Press®
A Division of Scholastic Inc.
New York / Toronto / London / Auckland / Sydney
Mexico City / New Delhi / Hong Kong
Danbury, Connecticut

Photo Credits: Cover © Fukuhara, Inc./Corbis; p. 5 © Pixland/Index Stock Imagery, Inc.; p. 7 © Bob Krist/Corbis; pp. 9, 11, 13, 15, 17, 19 © California Raisin Marketing Board; p. 21 © Benelux Press/Index Stock Imagery, Inc.

Contributing Editor: Shira Laskin
Book Design: Christopher Logan

Library of Congress Cataloging-in-Publication Data

Snyder, Inez.
    Grapes to raisins / by Inez Snyder.
    p. cm. — (How things are made)
    Includes index.
    ISBN 0-516-25198-8 (lib. bdg.) — ISBN 0-516-25528-2 (pbk.)
    1. Fruit—Drying—Juvenile literature. 2. Grapes—Juvenile literature. 3. Raisins
—Juvenile literature. I. Title. II. Series.

TX612.F7S55 2005
641.3'48—dc22

                                                          2004010334

5 6 7 8 9 10 R 14 13 12 11 10

Contents

These are **raisins**.

Raisins are made
from grapes.

5

Grapes grow on **vines**.

People pick the grapes when they are **ripe**.

7

After the grapes are picked, they are put on paper **trays** in the Sun.

The Sun begins to dry the grapes.

9

Next, the trays of grapes are rolled up.

The grapes must dry like this for a few days.

Now the grapes are raisins.

13

The raisins are put into a **machine**.

The machine takes the **stems** off of the raisins.

15

Next, the raisins are checked by another machine.

The bad raisins are taken out.

Now the raisins are washed.

Then they are packed into boxes and sent to stores.

Raisins are used in many foods.

New Words

machine (**muh**-sheen) something that is made to do work or to help make other things

raisins (**ray**-zuhnz) sweet fruits that come from grapes that have been dried

ripe (**ripe**) ready to be picked, harvested, or eaten

stems (**stemz**) the parts of plants that the leaves, flowers, and fruits are attached to

trays (**trays**) flat containers used to carry or hold things

vines (**vinez**) plants with long stems that grow along the ground

To Find Out More

Books
Grapes
by Robert B. Noyed
The Child's World, Inc.

How Do You Raise a Raisin?
by Pam Muñoz Ryan
Charlesbridge Publishing, Inc.

Web Site
California Raisins Rock!
http://www.calraisins.org/education
This Web site has fun games, raisin recipes, and directions
for drying your own raisins.

Index

About the Author
Inez Snyder writes books to help children learn how to read.

Content Consultant
Barry Shaffer, Area Business Management Extension Educator, Lake Erie Regional Grape Program

Reading Consultants
Kris Flynn, Coordinator, Small School District Literacy, The San Diego County Office of Education

Shelly Forys, Certified Reading Recovery Specialist, W.J. Zahnow Elementary School, Waterloo, IL

Paulette Mansell, Certified Reading Recovery Specialist, and Early Literacy Consultant, TX